STOCK MARKET ESSENTIALS

Unlocking the Basics, Making Informed Choices and Building Your Wealth

Richard Miller

Copyright

Table of content

INTRODUCTION

Welcome to stock market basics: Uncover the basics, make informed decisions, and build wealth In the ever-evolving personal finance landscape, the stock market is a formidable force.

It is also an unparalleled path to wealth creation.

This book is your compass, guiding you through the basic principles, strategic insights, and innovative knowledge you need to walk the path to financial mastery.

Demystifying the Basics These pages demystify the stock market, which is often seen as a complex area reserved for financial experts.

We embark on a journey to unravel the fundamentals, from understanding market dynamics to understanding the importance of risk management.

Whether you are a novice investor or looking to strengthen your financial acumen, this section will lay the foundation for a comprehensive understanding of the stock market.

Make Informed Decisions With vast investment opportunities, making informed decisions is key.

The book serves as a guide to a variety of investment vehicles, providing insight into stocks, bonds, real estate, cryptocurrencies, and more.

We dig deep into the art of strategic decision-making and help you align your investments with your personal financial goals.

As you read each chapter, you will gain the knowledge you need to approach the decisions before you with confidence and clarity.

Build Wealth After all, the stock market is more than just a place to store capital.

It is a dynamic arena for wealth creation.
Explore strategies to equip yourself with the essentials, build a resilient portfolio, maintain disciplined investment habits, and navigate financial ups and downs.
The journey to building lasting wealth is about more than numbers.
It's about empowering yourself to build a financial future that fulfills your aspirations and dreams.
As you embark on this adventure with Stock Market Essentials, imagine it as more than just a book, but a companion on your transformational journey to financial empowerment.
These page principles are not static.
They catalyze action, guide you through the dynamic landscape of the stock market, and set the stage for a financially prosperous future.
Open the door to financial wisdom, make informed decisions that align with

your goals, and get ready to start on the path to building lasting wealth.

The journey begins now - let's overcome financial limitations together.

Chapter 1

"Introduction to Financial Markets"

Welcome to the exciting and dynamic world of financial markets.

It's where wealth is created, where economic conditions are shaped, and where individuals like you can embark on a journey to build lasting wealth.

This foundational chapter delves deep into the heart of the stock market, uncovering its secrets and understanding its central role in the broader financial ecosystem.

The Attraction of the Stock Market, also known as the engine of capitalism, functions as a marketplace where buyers and sellers exchange ownership of companies.

This is a fascinating area where companies can go public, and issue shares to the public, and investors like you can become shareholders and share in their success.

Think of this market as a bustling city with a variety of shops lining the streets.

Each share represents ownership in a company and offers investors the opportunity to participate in the company's growth and profitability.

The appeal lies in the potential for capital appreciation, dividends, and the thrill of being part of a company that shapes an industry and economy.

Understanding the Basics

Understanding the basics is key to navigating this complex market.

Stocks, bonds, and other financial instruments are components of markets.

Stocks, also known as stocks, represent ownership in a company, while bonds represent debt issued by a company or government.

These products, along with a variety of derivatives, form a diverse and interconnected financial ecosystem.

We investigate the function of stock exchanges where buyers and sellers come together to set prices through the forces of supply and demand.

Prominent exchanges such as the New York Stock Exchange (NYSE) and Nasdaq are the hubs of financial activity in the world.

These hold stocks of well-known companies and serve as a barometer of the health of the economy.

The Market as a Mirror of Economic Reality The stock market is more than a realm of profit and loss.

It is a mirror that reflects economic reality.

Economic indicators such as gross domestic product (GDP), unemployment rate, and interest rates influence market movements.

A closer look at these interrelated dynamics provides insight into how global events, political decisions, and economic changes influence the rise and fall of markets.

The Language of Finance This chapter introduces the language of finance and demystifies terms such as market capitalization, dividends, and earnings per share.

Understanding these concepts is important to making informed decisions and navigating your financial situation with confidence.

The Path to Wealth Creation As we embark on this journey, let us consider this chapter about the path to the world of wealth creation.

Whether you're a novice investor or someone looking to deepen their understanding, the insights you'll gain here will provide the foundation for a successful and rewarding entry into the stock market.

Probably.

Open the door to financial opportunity and get ready to embark on a path that could change your financial future.

The journey begins now!

Evolution of Financial Markets To truly understand the importance of the stock market, let's go back in time.

Learn the historical development of financial markets, from the first stock exchange in Amsterdam to today's global network of interconnected markets.

Understanding this evolution provides valuable context and shows how stock markets have adapted and thrived over centuries of economic change and technological advancement.

Market Participants and Their Roles

When delving deeper into the world of financial markets, it is important to be aware of the diverse cast of characters that play important roles.

All participants contribute to market dynamics, from individual investors like you to institutional investors, market makers, and regulators.

See how these players interact, influence prices and together shape market development.

Psychological Aspects of Investing

Investing is more than just a numbers game.

It is a journey influenced by human emotions, market sentiments, and behavioral patterns.

Discover the psychological side of investing and learn how fear, greed, and herd psychology influence decision-making.

With this knowledge, you will be able to deal with market fluctuations and make informed and rational decisions even when faced with emotional challenges.

Market Trends and Cycles Markets are dynamic entities characterized by trends and cycles that influence investment strategies.

Delve deep into the concepts of bull and bear markets to understand the forces driving upward momentum and the inevitable corrections that accompany them.

Gaining insight into technical analysis and chart patterns will help you identify potential opportunities and manage risks effectively.

Regulatory Status Regulators play an important role in maintaining the integrity and fairness of financial markets.

Explore the regulatory landscape governing stock markets, from securities commissions to market oversight organizations.

Understanding the rules and regulations allows us to operate within a framework that promotes transparency, investor protection, and market stability.

Technological advances and trading platforms In the digital age, technology has changed the way we interact with financial markets.

Discover the impact of algorithmic trading, electronic communication networks (ECNs), and online securities platforms.

Learn how advances in technology have democratized access to the stock market, giving investors unprecedented tools and resources to execute trades and manage their portfolios.

Setting Investment Goals Before you begin your investment journey, it is important to define your financial goals.

Consider a variety of investment goals, from short-term profits to long-term wealth creation, and customize them to suit your risk tolerance and time horizon.

This chapter will help you build a solid foundation for your investment strategy and ensure that every financial decision contributes to your overall goals.

Conclusion By completing the comprehensive review in Chapter 1, you have laid the foundation for a thorough understanding of the stock market.

With historical insight, knowledge of market participants, a sense of psychological nuance, and awareness of technological advances, you'll be ready to dig deeper into your next chapter.

The road ahead promises financial empowerment and a strategic approach to unlocking the huge potential of the stock market.

Get ready for the next chapter as we delve into the practicalities of starting your journey to building lasting wealth and making informed decisions.

Chapter 2

"Starting Investing"

Welcome to the gateway to financial self-determination!

In this chapter, you will embark on a journey of self-discovery and strategic planning as you take your first steps into the world of investing.

Understanding how to start investing is key to making your financial goals a reality, whether it's your dream vacation, your children's education, or saving for your ideal retirement.

Your investment journey begins Think of your financial journey as a road trip.

Before you set out, you'll need your destination, a reliable vehicle, and a road map.

Similarly, your investment journey begins by defining your financial goals.

Are you looking for short-term profits, long-term wealth creation, or both?

Identifying your goals provides a compass to guide your investment decisions.

Create an Investment Plan: After setting your goals, the next step is to create an investment plan.

This includes assessing your risk tolerance, which is a key factor in determining the composition of assets within your portfolio.

We explore how to find the right balance of risk and return, ensuring your investment plan meets your comfort level while maximizing your growth potential.

The Importance of Diversification: Think of your investment portfolio like a garden.

Just as a diverse garden with a variety of plants is more resistant to pests and diseases, a diversified investment portfolio is more resistant to market fluctuations.

Understand the importance of diversification and spread your investments across different asset classes to reduce risk and increase stability.

Investment Vehicles: Stocks, Bonds, etc.

Now that you have your investment plan in place, it's time to consider different ways to achieve your financial goals.

Immerse yourself in the world of stocks, bonds, mutual funds, and exchange-traded funds (ETFs).

Understand how each investment vehicle works, what its risk and return profile is, and how they can complement each other in a balanced portfolio.

Setting Up an Investment Account Just as you need the right tools for a road trip, you need the right account for your investment journey.

Explore different types of investment accounts, from individual brokerage accounts to tax-advantaged accounts like IRAs and 401(k)s.

Learn how to use these accounts strategically to minimize taxes and maximize investment returns.

The Power of Compound Interest: One of the most attractive aspects of investing is the power of compound interest.

Think of your formulation like a snowball rolling down a hill.

It increases in force and size as time passes.

Understand how reinvesting your earnings accelerates the growth of your investments and turns small donations into great wealth over time.

Make regular posting a habit

Consistency is the driving force of your investment journey.

Understand the importance of contributing regularly to your investment account, regardless of market conditions.

We explore the concept of dollar-cost averaging.

This is a strategy where you invest a fixed amount on a regular basis, which helps smooth out market volatility and increase your overall returns.

Conclusion After completing the detailed discussion in Chapter 2, you have laid the foundation for successful investing.

You've defined your financial goals, created a personalized investment plan, explored different investment vehicles, set up the right account, and harnessed the power of compound interest.

The road ahead of you is paved with opportunities to increase your wealth, and you now have the knowledge and confidence to navigate it effectively.

Let's break down Chapter 2 into practical steps to give you practical advice to get started investing.

1.Define your financial goals: Action steps: Clarify your short-term and long-term financial goals.

Quantify your goals, such as saving for a down payment, funding your child's education, or building a home for retirement.

2.Assess your risk tolerance: Action steps: Take the risk tolerance assessment quiz available on many investment platforms.

Think about how comfortable you are with market fluctuations and potential losses.

3.Create an Investment Plan: Action Step: Create a written investment plan that outlines your goals, risk tolerance, and the types of investments you are considering.

Decide how much to allocate to different asset classes (stocks, bonds, etc.) based on your risk tolerance and financial goals.

4.Understanding Diversification: Action Steps: Research and identify diverse investments across different sectors and industries.

For broader market exposure, consider investing in index funds or ETFs.

5.Research investment products: Action Step: Open a brokerage account with a reputable platform.

Start with low-cost, beginner-friendly investment options like index funds and mutual funds.

6.Setting Up an Investment Account: Action Step: Open a tax-advantaged account, such as an Individual Retirement Account (IRA) or a workplace 401(k).

Enjoy tax benefits and optimize your investment strategy with these accounts.

7.Harness the Power of Compound Interest: Action Step: Reinvest dividends and interest from your investments.

Deposit additional funds regularly to take full advantage of compound interest.

8.Get in the habit of making regular contributions: Action Step: Set up automatic contributions to your investment account.

Consistency is key.

Set up a monthly giving routine that fits your budget.

9.Stay Informed: Action Steps: Read books, attend webinars, and follow trusted financial news sources to stay informed.

Understand the basics of financial statements and key financial indicators to make informed investment decisions.

10.Monitoring and Adjustment: Action Step: Periodically review the performance of your portfolio and rebalance as necessary.

If your financial situation or goals change significantly, adjust your investment plan.

11.Research Specific Investments: Action Step: Take a closer look at specific stocks, bonds, or funds that fit your investment plan.

Understand the companies and assets you're investing in by considering factors such as financial health, growth prospects, and management.

12.Leverage investment tools and resources: Action step: Explore the analytical tools of your chosen securities platform.

Make informed investment decisions using financial calculators, stock screeners, and research reports.

13.Have Patience and Discipline: Action Steps: Resist the urge to react impulsively to short-term market fluctuations.

Develop a long-term mindset and stay true to your investment strategy.

14.Learn from your mistakes: Action steps: Accept that not all investment decisions will be perfect.

Analyze losses and underperforming investments to learn and improve your approach.

15.Consider expert advice:

Action steps:

If you would like tailored advice based on your financial situation, please contact a financial advisor.

Understand the fees associated with professional advice and choose an advisor whose philosophy aligns with your goals.

16.Build your emergency savings: Action Step: Before you get serious about investing, make sure you have an emergency fund.

Make sure you can cover three to six months' worth of living expenses in a liquid, easily accessible account.

17.Stay informed about tax implications: Action steps: Understand the tax implications of your investments.

Be aware of capital gains taxes, dividends, and how each account is taxed differently.

18.Reinvest unexpected funds and bonuses: Action Step: If you receive unexpected funds, consider allocating some of them to your investment portfolio.

This could include a tax refund, a work bonus, or an unexpected gift.

19.Network and Learn from Others: Action Steps: Join investment forums and local investment clubs to connect with like-minded people.

Share your experiences and insights and learn from the successes and challenges of others.

20.Review and update your plan regularly: Action Step: Schedule regular check-ins to review your investment plan.

Update your goals, risk tolerance, and strategy as your financial situation changes.

By following these practical steps, you will not only build a solid foundation for your investment journey, but you will also become an active participant in the wealth creation process.

Remember that investing is a lifelong learning experience and each step brings you closer to achieving your financial goals.

Stay disciplined, stay informed, and enjoy your journey to building lasting wealth.

Chapter 3

"Deciphering Stocks and Bonds"

Welcome to the heart of your investment journey!

This chapter unravels the complex world of stocks and bonds and provides you with a comprehensive understanding of these fundamental investment vehicles.

A closer look at the inner workings of stocks and bonds provides insight into how they work, the risks and rewards associated with them, and how to strategically integrate them into your investment portfolio.

Understanding Stocks: Percentage Ownership What are Stocks?

Essentially, stocks represent ownership in a company.

When you own stock, you own a portion of a company's assets and earnings.

It's like you are a partner in a company and your wealth increases and decreases with the success of the company.

Actionable Insights: Research a company and understand its business model, competitive advantages, and financial health before investing.

Consider investing in established companies with consistent performance.

Risk and Reward: Stocks have significant upside potential, but they also come with high volatility.

Diversification helps reduce the risks associated with individual stocks.

Exploring Bonds: The World of Bonds

What are Bonds?

Unlike stocks, bonds represent debt.

When you invest in a bond, you are essentially lending money to a company or government in exchange for periodic interest payments and repayment of the principal at maturity.

Practical Insights: Understand the different types of bonds, including government, corporate, and municipal bonds.

Consider the bond's credit rating, which indicates the issuer's creditworthiness.

Risk and Return: Bonds provide stable income through interest payments.

Although bond prices are considered safer than stocks, they can still fluctuate due to interest rates and credit risk.

Dynamic Duo: Building a Balanced Portfolio Balancing Method: A balanced approach aimed at optimizing returns while managing risk by combining stocks and bonds within a portfolio will be created.

The ratio of stocks to bonds depends on your risk tolerance, time horizon, and financial goals.

Practical Insight: Adjust your portfolio regularly to maintain the desired asset allocation.

Consider age-based strategies like the "100 minus age" rule as a starting point for stock allocation.

Working with Market Indices and ETFs

Market Indices: Market indices, such as the S&P 500, track the performance of specific groups of stocks and provide a measure of market performance.

Understanding indexes can help you assess how well your investments are performing compared to the broader market.

Exchange Traded Funds (ETFs): ETFs are mutual funds that hold a basket of stocks, bonds, or other assets and provide instant diversification.

ETFs trade on exchanges and provide liquidity and flexibility for investors.

Practical Insights: Use ETFs to gain exposure to specific sectors, industries, or geographic regions.

To minimize costs, do your research and choose an ETF with a low expense ratio.

Analyzing Financial Statements

Fundamental Analysis: Fundamental analysis evaluates a company's financial statements to assess its health and growth potential.

The most important financial statements include the income statement, balance sheet, and cash flow statement.

Practical Insights: Aim for consistent sales and profit growth.

Assess a company's debt levels and liquidity.

Risk Management Strategies

Diversification and Asset Allocation: Diversify across different asset classes, industries, and geographic regions.

Adjust your asset allocation based on changing financial and market conditions.
Practical Insight: Review and rebalance your portfolio regularly to maintain diversification.
Allocate assets based on investment goals, risk tolerance, and time horizon.

Advanced Strategies:

Options and Derivatives Options Trading: Options give the right, but not the obligation, to buy or sell an asset at a predetermined price.
Options can be used for hedging, income generation, or speculation.
Practical Insights: Understand the risks associated with options trading, including the potential for significant loss.
Consider your options strategy based on your risk tolerance and market outlook.

Behavioral Finance: Master Investment Psychology Emotional Intelligence: Recognize the emotional aspects of investing, such as fear, greed, and overconfidence.

Develop emotional intelligence to make rational decisions during market fluctuations.

Practical Insights: Stick to your investment plan and avoid impulsive decisions based on short-term market movements.

Maintain a disciplined approach by regularly assessing your emotions and biases.

ESG Investing: Aligning Investments with Values Environmental, Social, and Governance (ESG) Standards: ESG investing incorporates ethical, social, and environmental factors into investment decisions.

Investors align their portfolios with companies that prioritize sustainability and social responsibility.

Actionable insights: Research companies with strong ESG practices.

Choose ESG funds and stocks that align with your values and long-term goals.

Tax-Efficient Investment Strategies Tax Savings Planning: Understand the tax implications of your investment decisions.

Use tax-efficient strategies to minimize capital gains and optimize your after-tax returns.

Practical Insight: Consider recovering losses to offset profits and losses.

Explore tax-advantaged accounts to maximize your tax benefits.

Global Diversification and Emerging Markets Global Opportunities: Diversify your Portfolio by Investing in International Markets Emerging markets have the potential for growth but come with higher risks.

Practical Insights: Explore global economic trends and geopolitical factors.

Allocate a portion of your portfolio to international or emerging market funds.

Continuously Learn and Adapt Stay informed: Financial markets are dynamic.

Stay informed about economic trends, political changes, and world events.

Continually learn about new investment opportunities and strategies.

Actionable Insights: Follow trusted financial news sources and industry publications.

Attend workshops, webinars, and conferences to stay up-to-date on market trends.

After completing this in-depth exploration of Chapter 3, you will have explored advanced investment strategies, mastered the psychology of investing, and explored how to align your investments with your values.

We have practical insight and a comprehensive understanding of financial products to help you navigate the complexities of the ever-evolving financial landscape.

Remember that investing is a dynamic journey and adaptability is key.

Stay curious, stay informed, and embrace the continuous learning process.

Upcoming chapters will further enhance your investment toolkit and provide actionable strategies for building and protecting your wealth.

Your financial adventure continues and the possibilities are endless.

Get ready to move on to the next chapter.

Here you'll find practical tips to help you make informed investment decisions and stay financially successful.

Chapter 4

"Reading Financials"

Welcome to the complex world of financial analysis and market indicators.

In this chapter, we embark on a fascinating journey through the vast landscape of financial reports, metrics, and key indicators that provide valuable insight into the health of companies and the broader economy.

Improving your skills at deciphering these financial signals will help you make informed investment decisions and navigate the ever-changing tides of the market.

Decoding Financial Statements Income Statement: Learn how the income statement reveals a company's revenue, expenses, and profitability.

Understand key metrics such as earnings per share (EPS) and net income to evaluate financial performance.

Balance Sheet: Discover the secrets of the balance sheet, which shows a company's assets, liabilities, and equity.

Learn how to assess liquidity, solvency, and overall financial stability.

Cash Flow Statement: Delve into the intricacies of the cash flow statement and shed light on a company's cash flow-generating activities.

Assess a company's ability to meet its obligations and fund future growth.

Financial Ratios: Analysis Toolkit

Liquidity Ratios: Understand metrics such as current ratios and quick ratios to assess a company's short-term liquidity.

Learn how these metrics indicate a company's ability to meet short-term obligations.

Profitability: Analyze profitability such as return on equity (ROE) and profit margin.

Gain insight into how efficiently your company is using its resources to generate profits.

Debt Ratios: Learn about debt-to-equity ratios, interest coverage ratios, and other ratios for evaluating a company's leverage.

Evaluates a company's ability to manage its debt and pay interest.

Market Indicators: Navigating the Economic Situation Gross Domestic Product (GDP): Discover the importance of GDP as a barometer of economic health.

Understand how GDP growth or decline affects investment decisions.

Unemployment Rate: Investigates the impact of the unemployment rate on consumer spending and corporate profitability.

Recognize the relationship between employment trends and the stock market.

Interest Rates: Unraveling the role of interest rates in investment decisions.

Understand how changes in interest rates affect different asset classes such as stocks and bonds.

Earnings Reports and Guidance

Analyzing Earnings Reports: Learn how to interpret quarterly and annual earnings reports from companies.

Identify key elements of the report, such as revenue growth, revenue surprises, and future projections.

Management Guidance: Understand the importance of management guidance in predicting a company's future performance.

Evaluate the reliability of guidance and its impact on stock prices.

Technical Analysis: Market Trend Charts

Chart Patterns: Discover common chart

patterns such as head and shoulders charts, triangles, and double tops.

Understand how technical analysts use these patterns to predict future price movements.

Moving Averages: Analyze moving averages as a tool to identify trends and potential reversal points.

Gain insight into the role of moving averages in smoothing out price fluctuations.

Revised Risk Management Strategies

Stop Loss Orders: Learn More How stop loss orders can help protect your investments from significant losses.

Implement stop-loss orders as part of a disciplined risk management strategy.

Position Sizing: Consider the concept of position sizing to determine the appropriate capital allocation for each investment.

Reduce risk through diversification across different asset classes and individual securities.

World Economic Indicators: Macro View Purchasing Managers Index (PMI): Understand how the PMI reflects manufacturing and economic activity.

PMI is used as a leading indicator of economic trends.

Consumer Confidence Index: Explore the importance of consumer confidence in predicting spending patterns.

Evaluate how changes in consumer sentiment affect the stock market.

By the end of Chapter 4's comprehensive discussion, you will have covered the complete picture of financial reports, ratios, and market indicators.

You now have analytical tools to analyze your company's finances, interpret economic indicators, and navigate complex technical analysis.

With this knowledge, you will be better equipped to make informed investment decisions and adapt to the ever-changing dynamics of the financial world.

In the next chapter, we will look at practical strategies for applying this knowledge to your investment approach.

Get ready to learn practical techniques for building and managing your investment portfolio as you continue your journey to financial success.

It's up to you to master the complexities of your financial environment, and the opportunities to make informed decisions are endless.

The adventure in the world of finance continues!

Chapter 5

"Mastering Risk Management on Your Investment Journey"

Welcome to the critical area of risk management, the foundation of successful investing.

This chapter describes viable strategies and practical approaches to protect your portfolio from potential pitfalls.

As you navigate a complex risk environment, you'll gain insight into how to effectively identify, measure, and mitigate risk to ensure your investment journey recovers in the face of uncertainty.

1.Risk Assessment: Know Your Risk Tolerance and Goals Action Steps: Understand your risk tolerance by conducting a thorough self-assessment.

Align your risk tolerance with your investment goals, time horizon, and financial goals.

Practical Insight: Understand that investing involves risk and that different people have different levels of comfort.

Set clear goals so you can tailor your risk management strategy to your unique situation.

2.Diversification: Spread risk across all assets Action Step: Diversify your portfolio across different asset classes, industries, and geographic regions.

Avoid concentration risk by not committing too much to a single investment or sector.

Practical Insight: Diversification reduces the impact of poorly performing assets on the overall portfolio.

Regularly evaluate and rebalance your portfolio to maintain effective diversification.

3.Asset Allocation: Balancing Risk and Reward Action Steps: Determine the appropriate asset mix based on your risk tolerance and investment goals.

Adjust your asset allocation as financial and market conditions change.

Practical Insights: Asset allocation is a dynamic process.

You need to adapt to changing circumstances and market trends.

Finding the right balance between stocks, bonds, and other assets is important for effective risk management.

4.Stop Loss Order: Tactical Tool to Reduce Risk Action Step: Set a predetermined stop loss level for an investment.

Review your stop-loss orders regularly and adjust them based on market conditions and risk tolerance needs.

Practical Insight: A stop-loss order prevents significant losses by automatically triggering a sale when an investment reaches a specified decline.

Use stop-loss orders in conjunction with other risk management strategies for a comprehensive approach.

5.Emergency Fund: Safety Net for Financial Stability Action Steps: Maintain an emergency fund equal to three to six months of living expenses.

Keep your emergency fund liquid and easily accessible.

Practical Insights: An emergency fund provides a financial cushion and reduces the need to liquidate investments in unforeseen circumstances.

Regularly review and update your emergency fund based on changes in your financial situation.

6.Hedging: Mitigate Specific Risks Action Steps: Use financial instruments such as options and futures to hedge specific risks.
Understand the costs and benefits of hedging strategies relative to your overall investment objectives.

Practical Insights: Hedging allows you to protect your portfolio against adverse market movements and certain risks associated with particular assets.

Please consider seeking professional advice before implementing any complex hedging strategy.

7.Regular Portfolio Reviews: Be Proactive Action Steps: Schedule regular reviews of your investment portfolio.

Evaluate individual asset performance, overall portfolio performance, and changes in risk factors.

Practical Insights: Regular reviews help quickly identify and address emerging risks.

Stay aware of changes in economic conditions, market trends, and world events that may affect your investments.

8.Stay up to date with economic indicators.

Action Steps: Stay up to date on key economic indicators such as GDP, unemployment, and inflation.

Understand how these metrics impact different asset classes and your overall portfolio.

Practical Insights: Economic indicators provide valuable signals about possible changes in market conditions.

Adapt your investment strategy to evolving economic trends to effectively manage risk.

9.Scenario Planning: Forecasting and Preparation Action Steps: Create scenarios for different economic, market, or geopolitical conditions.

Create a contingency plan for each scenario to mitigate potential risks.

Practical Insights: Scenario planning helps you anticipate challenges and develop intentional responses.

Continuously update scenarios based on new trends and changing risk landscape.

10.Continuing Education: Empower Yourself Action Steps: Stay informed about new investment products, market trends, and risk management strategies.

Expand your knowledge by attending workshops, webinars, and conferences.

Practical Insights: The investment landscape continues to evolve.

Ongoing training keeps you ready for new challenges.

Networking with experts and other investors provides different perspectives and insights.

Conclusion By the end of this review of Chapter 5, you will have delved into the art of risk management and learned practical strategies for protecting and improving your investment portfolio.

Incorporating these actionable steps will not only strengthen your financial resilience but also enable you to make informed decisions in the face of uncertainty.

The next chapters continue to build on these risk management fundamentals and explore advanced techniques and strategies for optimizing your investment approach.

The road to economic prosperity continues, and the ability to effectively manage risk is a major advantage.

Prepare for the next stage of your investing adventure as you hone your skills and approach to building lasting wealth.

Chapter 6:

"Choosing the Right Investment: Navigating the Range of Options"

This important chapter begins with a detailed examination of various investment vehicles, each with its own characteristics, risks, and opportunities.

Our journey with mutual funds, exchange-traded funds (ETFs), and individual stocks is focused on helping you align your investment decisions with your personal goals.

Whether you seek diversification, passive exposure, or individual stock ownership, understanding these investment options is important to building a portfolio that reflects your financial goals.

1.Mutual Funds: Diversification Made Easy About Mutual Funds: Mutual funds pool money from multiple investors and invest in stocks, bonds, or other securities.

Invest in a diversified portfolio.

Perfect for investors looking for diversification without the need for extensive market research.

Target Adjustment: Select mutual funds based on investment objectives, growth, yield, or balanced approach.

Evaluate the fund manager's strategy and past performance.

Practical Considerations: Be aware of fees such as expense ratios and any opening or closing fees that may be incurred.

Periodically review your mutual fund holdings to ensure they are consistent with your evolving financial goals.

2.Exchange Traded Funds (ETFs): Flexibility and Low Costs About ETFs: ETFs are exchange-traded mutual funds that invest in assets such as stocks, bonds, and commodities.

represents a basket.

Similar to mutual funds, they offer instant diversification and flexibility.

Target Alignment: Select ETFs based on your investment strategy, such as sector-specific, thematic, or broad market exposure.

Consider low expense ratios that contribute to cost efficiency.

Practical Considerations: ETFs offer intraday trading and can be bought and sold throughout the trading day.

To minimize trading costs, consider commission-free ETF options offered by brokerage platforms.

3.Individual Stocks: Direct Ownership, Direct Determination Understanding Individual Stocks: Owning stock in a company means direct ownership of that company.

It provides the possibility of capital appreciation, dividends, and voting rights at shareholder meetings.

Target Alignment: Choose stocks based on your risk tolerance, investment horizon, and belief in a company's growth potential.

We thoroughly research companies, taking into account their financial health, competitive position, and industry trends.

Practical considerations: Diversify your stock portfolio and spread risk across different industries and sectors.

Stay informed about the companies you invest in by regularly checking financial reports and industry news.

4.Bonds: Bonds for Stability About Bonds: Bonds provide investors with stability in exchange for periodic interest payments and repayment of principal at maturity.

is a debt instrument that lends money to the issuer in exchange for earning income, and therefore suitable for conservative investors.

Target Adjustment: Choose a bond based on your risk tolerance and income needs.

We consider factors such as creditworthiness, term, and interest rate environment.

Practical Considerations: Understand the inverse relationship between bond prices and interest rates.

To manage credit risk, we spread our bond holdings across different issuers.

5.Real Estate: Tangible Assets for Long-Term Growth Understanding Real Estate Investing: Real estate investing includes owning physical real estate or investing in a real estate investment trust (REIT).

It offers rental income, capital appreciation, and the potential for portfolio diversification.

Target Adjustment: Choose your real estate investment based on your investment horizon, liquidity needs, and risk tolerance.

Consider factors such as location, property type, and market trends.

Practical Considerations: Evaluate the potential for rental income, property value appreciation, and associated costs.

REITs provide a liquid and diverse option for accessing real estate without directly owning it.

6.Precious Metals: Hedging Against Economic Uncertainty Understanding Precious Metal Investing: Precious metals, such as gold and silver, act as a hedge against inflation and economic uncertainty.

It can be held physically or through exchange-traded funds (ETFs) or mutual funds.

Target Adjustment: Consider precious metals as part of your portfolio for diversification and as a store of value.

Evaluate macroeconomic factors that can impact precious metal prices.

Practical Considerations: Understand the role of precious metals as a risk management tool in a balanced portfolio.

If you own physical precious metals, consider storage costs and accessibility.

7.Cryptocurrency: Emerging Digital Assets Understanding Cryptocurrency

Investing: Cryptocurrencies such as Bitcoin and Ethereum are digital assets that use blockchain technology.

High volatility, but potential for diversification and long-term growth.

Alignment with your goals: Approach investing in virtual currencies with caution, taking into account your risk tolerance and speculative nature.

Diversify your exposure to cryptocurrencies and stay informed of regulatory developments.

Practical considerations: Use a trusted cryptocurrency exchange for trading and storage.

Consider the long-term viability and use cases of a particular cryptocurrency.

8.Art and Collectibles: Tangible Investments with Aesthetic Appeal

Understanding Investing in Art and Collectibles: Art, Rare Coins, and

Collectibles Value Tangible Assets It can be an alternative investment for those who do.

Value is influenced by cultural significance, rarity, and market demand.

Target Target: Select art and collectibles based on personal interest and potential long-term value.

Please note that there are costs such as insurance and storage fees.

Practical Considerations: Consult a professional or appraiser to evaluate the value and authenticity of art and collectibles.

Understand the illiquidity of these investments and the potential challenges associated with resale.

Finally, To conclude this study In Chapter 6, we discussed various investment options that offer unique ways to build and expand your portfolio.

The path to lasting wealth requires carefully aligning these investment decisions to your personal goals, risk tolerance, and time horizon.

The next chapter provides more information on the psychology of financial planning, estate planning, and investing.

A comprehensive understanding of different investment vehicles will enable you to make informed decisions that promote financial success.

Get ready for the next stage of your investment adventure as you hone your strategies and unlock new dimensions of financial prosperity.

Chapter 7

"Creating a Financial Legacy: Timeless Strategies for Prosperity"

An in-depth look at the art and science of cultivating lasting wealth as we delve into the final chapters of financial transactions.

Let's embark on a journey together.

This chapter explains the complexities of building and maintaining wealth over the long term, providing insight into strategic portfolio adjustments, navigating market cycles with empathy, and the unwavering discipline required for financial success.

1. Long-Term Vision: Plan for Financial Success Goal Setting: Define long-term financial goals and set milestones for retirement, education, estate planning, etc.

I'll summarize.

Seamlessly align your investment strategy with these goals to drive a focused, methodical approach.

Practical Wisdom: Review and refine your financial goals regularly to ensure they evolve as your life changes, your economy changes, and your priorities change.

A carefully crafted roadmap serves as an unwavering guide to navigating the complexities of wealth creation.

Adapt to market changes and evolving financial needs to invest assets wisely across different classes.

2.Strategic Asset Mastery: Basic Principles of Portfolio Construction Aligning Risk and Return: Design a prudent strategic asset allocation plan that aligns with your risk tolerance, investment horizon, and financial goals.

Adapt to changing market conditions and changing financial needs by intelligently dividing your assets into different classes.

Practical Management: Rebalance your portfolio regularly to maintain your desired asset allocation.

Strategic asset management is the found ation for managing the ups and downs of market volatility.

3.Consistency as a Virtue: Harness the Power of Systematic Investing The Wonders of Dollar-Cost Averaging: Systematic Investing by Making Regular Contributions at Specifie d Intervals Run the program.

Take advantage of market fluctuations to accumulate more stocks during downturns.

Practical Wisdom: Systematic investing eliminates the need for market timing and instills a disciplined and unwavering approach.

Automated investment strategies establis h systematic savings habits.

4.Guardian of Wealth: The Art of Risk Management Continuous

Vigilance: Periodically evaluate portfolio performance, risk exposure, and alignment with financial objectives.

Adjust your risk management strategy as the market cha nges.

Practical Operations: Diversification, stop-loss orders, and other risk mitigation tools must be seamlessly integrated into an ongoing risk management strategy.

Be aware of potential risks and fluctuations that may affect portfolio performance.

5.Adjusting for Market Cycles: Navigating the Ups and Downs Understanding Economic and Market Dynamics: Stay informed about economic cycles, bull and bear markets, and overarching trends affecting asset valuations.

Adjust your investment strategy according to prevailing market conditions.

Practical Wisdom: Market
cycles present strategic opportunities.

Take advantage of the downturn and rea djust to the uptick.

Recognize the influence of market sentiment on short-term movements and guide long-term success based on fundamental principles.

6.Guardian of Discipline: Navigate Emotional Situations
Curb Emotional Decision Making: Use e motional intelligence to withstand market fluctuations and avoid impulsive d ecisions Let's feed it.

Stick to your investment plan and make decisions bas ed on logic, not reaction.

Practical Actions: Establish portfolio evaluation and adjustment routines to reduce the effects of emotional bias.

Recognize the important role of discipline and a steady, long-term approach to wealth creation.

7.Knowledge as Empowerment: A Lifelong Pursuit of Financial Literacy Adventures in Continuing Learning: Stay up to date on financial news, market trends, and evolving investment strategies.

Always educate yourself to make informed decisions and adapt to the fluidity of the financial landscape.

Practical
Wisdom: Deepen your understanding of f inancial markets with trusted financial literature, workshops, and conferences.

Your commitment to continuous learning will strengthen your financial capabilities.

8.Legacy Art: Creating a Secure Financial
Footprint Comprehensive Estate Planning: Create a comprehensive estate plan that aligns with your intentions and protects your assets for future generations.

Review and update your estate plan regularly to reflect changes in your financial situation and goals.

In Practice: When carefully planning your estate, consider the effects of taxes, inheritance laws, and family structure.

Seek expert advice to ensure resilience and direction in your estate planning.

9.Tax Efficiency Choreography: Maximizing After-Tax Profits Strategic Tax Symphony: Employ tax-efficient investment strategies to reduce the impact of taxes on profits.

Find tax-advantaged accounts and use tax-efficient investment vehicles.

Practical Wisdom: Understand the tax implications of various investment decisions, including capital gains, dividends, and interest income.

Regularly review and improve your tax strategy in response to changes in tax law and your financial situation.

10.Iterative Excellence:
The Eternal Cycle of Review and Adjustment Portfolio Alchemy: Periodically review your investment portfolio to ensure that your goals and risk tolerance are aligned.

Make adjustments based on the ever-changing interplay of financial conditions, market trends, and economic outlook.

Practical Operations: Regular evaluation ensures that your portfolio is dynamic, responsive, and optimally balanced.

An iterative process of review and adjustment is essential to maintaining a sharp and balanced portfolio.

Finally, By completing this adventure up to Chapter 7, you will have learned a range of timeless strategies for building and maintaining wealth.

The principles of long-term vision, strategic asset management, disciplined investing, and continuous learning are the foundation for lasting financial success.

Armed with these insights, you will be better equipped to navigate the maze of the financial landscape, adapt to changing market conditions, and achieve lasting prosperity.

Conclusion

"Stock Market Basics: Navigate Your Path to Financial Mastery"

As we bring the curtain down on our exploration into the intricate world of the stock market within the pages of "Stock Market Essentials: Unlocking the Basics, Making Informed Choices, and Building Your Wealth," it's not just a conclusion, it is a transition and the beginning of a new and powerful stage in your financial journey.

The journey we took together through these pages was more than just a journey of words.

It was an invitation to dig deeper into stock market fundamentals.

From the basics of market dynamics to unraveling the intricacies of various investment vehicles, this book aims to help you not only understand the nuances but also make informed decisions to achieve your personal financial goals.

It's about equipping yourself with important tools to make decisions.

By covering the basics, you have built a solid foundation in understanding the complexities of markets, risk management techniques, and the strategic approach required to make successful investments.

Making informed decisions is key to navigating the maze of investment options, from stocks and bonds to real estate and cryptocurrencies.

The last page of this book is more than just the end of a chapter.

They represent a new beginning, a new chapter with key insights to make informed decisions, and the beginning of a journey to lasting financial prosperity.

"Building wealth" is not a single step, but a continuous and eternal endeavor.

The principles described in these pages - discipline, continuous learning, and strategic acumen - are more than just theoretical constructs; they are benchmarks that will guide you on your path to sustained financial success.

The stock market is a dynamic ecosystem with ups and downs, and the ability to adapt, learn, and persevere will be central to your financial journey.

Prepare to move from theory to practice and prepare for a journey marked by prudence, resilience, and the unwavering pursuit of financial goals.

Your wealth-building journey goes beyond these written words.

Every financial decision you make is a stroke on the canvas of your financial legacy.

Stock Market Essentials is more than just a book.

It is an invitation to a transformative journey that opens the door to financial empowerment, makes informed and goal-aligned decisions, and continually builds wealth that will pave the way to the life you envision.

May your financial adventure lead to growth, prosperity, and the realization of your dreams.

Your continued journey to lasting wealth and financial mastery is here.

On this journey, the knowledge you gain in these pages will become a catalyst for a future of financial abundance and empowerment.